DOWNLOAD THESE 50 PROMPTS FREE TODAY

Instantly Boost Your Productivity & Drive More Sales With These 50+ Free AI Prompts

This is the ultimate list of AI prompts created by real marketing professionals to power their online business. Use these prompts to drive more sales, generate more traffic, and ultimately become more productive overnight.

Download Your 50 Free Prompts

www.tend2business.com/ai-prompts

Table Of Contents

Introduction AI AFFILIATE MARKETING

In this book we're going to show you how to use AI for affiliate marketing.

So, let's dive in now. What is AI affiliate marketing? Let's start with affiliate marketing. You tell your friends, family, or maybe even place ads about a product because you believe in it so much. And here's the cool part: if someone buys that product because of what you said or advertised, you get some money as a reward. So, it's a way to make money by promoting products you love. That's what affiliate marketing is all about!

The difference here is now you can use AI tools for your affiliate marketing, and this makes things so much faster and better and that it's pretty much revolutionizing the way you do affiliate marketing. Why? Because it's very easy to start. In the

past there's always been an issue with where to start. There's so much to do such as creating content. All these things get pretty much solved because of these AI tools that we're going to talk about in this course.

It's very data-driven so no longer do you have to throw things out there and see if it works. Because the data is available. You could actually see what works and what doesn't work. Then tailor your campaign based around that data. That saves you a lot of time. It's very fast because of the amount of content you can create, and the number of things you can do. You are no longer staring at a blank screen trying to figure out where to get started. These AI tools help you to get started super-fast.

Now what can you do with AI? Well, these AI tools expedite your results. So, you can start creating the landing copy. You no longer have to worry about things like what do I write, what should my headline be, what type of description I should put on it, or what should a button say.

Landing page creation is a very important task for building your e-mail list and capturing your customer information. AI can help you do that. AI can help you write the content for your landing page, design your ads including your ad copy and the graphics for the ad.

You could also do e-mail follow-ups. This is the part that gets missed most of the time when it comes to affiliate marketing, but e-mail follow-ups are very very important. That's where the majority of the sales happened. And I know, even I have done this where I look at a blank screen and I don't know what to write or my e-mail feels so boring. Well AI fixes that problem because it can give you the e-mail to send out and we're going to show you how to do that. We're going to show you exactly what tools to use to create these emails.

Last but not least, you could also use AI to reach organic social media traffic so that you could start putting your products out there and get traffic to the landing pages. You can use social media traffic to drive sales and we're gonna cover all of this within this book. I'm excited to dive in, let's get started.

Chapter 1 Secret # 1 AI for Landing Page Copy: Hooks and Copy

In this secret we're going to show you how to use AI tools for your landing page copy creation. Let's get started!

There are multiple elements for the landing page that you can create using AI.

First thing that you would always need on a landing page is a headline or some sort of hook that grabs people's attention as soon as they land on your page.

The other thing you're going to need is a sub headline to deliver more detail of what you're talking about.

Then the copy of the landing page - you're going to write a description of what you're offering, a lead magnet, maybe you're giving something away of value so that you collect your customers' information. This could be name, e-mail, or phone number.

This all can be created for your landing page using the AI tools that we're about to show you.

If you're giving something away of value that's called a lead magnet. Then you're going to have to deliver that item. For 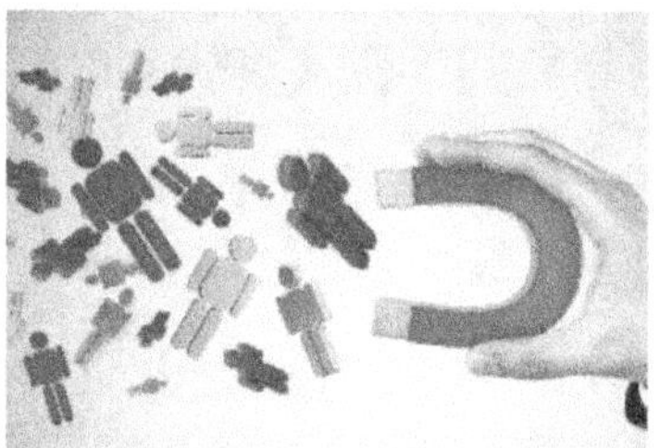 that you can use a thank you page. And you're gonna welcome them on the thank you page and then have your links in there to say thank you for signing up for my e-mail list and here's exactly the report that I promised you or the video I promised you.

You're going to create a thank you page for that.

All this copy can be written using AI. I'm going to show you a very simple way using a free tool. We're going to be using ChatGpt.

It's been around now for a little bit and a lot of people get confused and it's still fairly new, so I'll give you exact prompts to use to start creating all the elements for your landing page, Ok?

To try ChatGpt if you don't have an account, just go create a free account. All the examples you're going to see here are going to be using the free version. I'm not paying for any of it.

I'm giving it a prompt and I'm showing you what it came up with as well. Then we're going to work through the same example throughout all the secrets. Follow along and you could use the same prompts. Change it for the product that you're promoting and just start creating the content. You must take action in order for this to work for you.

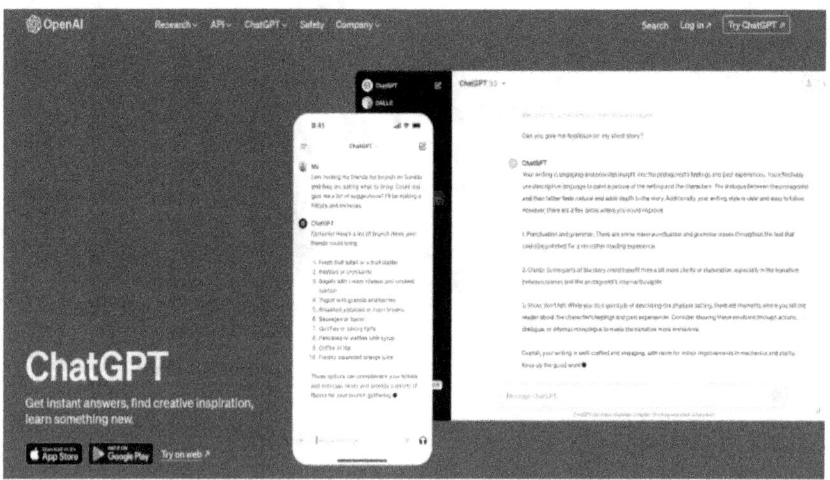

So...hooks and headline. You're now going to create a hook and a headline for your landing page. What should your ChatGPT prompt be? Feel free to copy and paste the prompt ChatGpt. I wrote *"Could you please give me 5 headline and book ideas for my new product called AI Affiliate Marketing."* Since AI affiliate marketing is this product, I just went ahead and used that. If you're promoting different products; weight loss offers, your own product or whatever it is, go ahead and put that in there. Substitute. It doesn't have to be 5 headlines. It could be 10. It could be 3. That's up to you. Side note: I always say could you please and I say my please and thank you so if you don't want to use that you know that's OK.

Now I know there's been lots of complicated prompts out there where people say could you act like this, could you be loud, or could pretend to be this. You could absolutely use those prompts. However, here I'm showing you that you could just ask it a simple question as a conversation. One like: *"Could you please give me five headlines for my new product called AI Affiliate Marketing."* And it gives you the exact same answer. I think it works perfectly fine. You don't need to complicate things.

I went ahead and pasted this prompt within ChatGpt and the picture that you see here.

Certainly! Here are five book ideas along with their headlines for your new product "AI Affiliate Marketing":

1. **Book Title:** "AI Affiliate Marketing: The Complete Guide"
   * **Headline:** "Master the Art of Affiliate Marketing with Artificial Intelligence"
2. **Book Title:** "AI Affiliate Marketing Secrets Unveiled"
   * **Headline:** "Unlocking the Hidden Potential of AI in Affiliate Marketing"
3. **Book Title:** "Profitable Partnerships: AI and Affiliate Marketing"
   * **Headline:** "A Deep Dive into AI-Enhanced Affiliate Marketing Strategies"
4. **Book Title:** "Affiliate Success in the AI Era"
   * **Headline:** "Harnessing AI for Unprecedented Affiliate Marketing Profits"
5. **Book Title:** "AI Affiliate Marketing Playbook"
   * **Headline:** "Your Roadmap to Profitable Affiliate Marketing with Artificial Intelligence"

These are the five prompts that it came back with. You have to keep in mind sometimes ChatGpt has a good day, sometimes it has a bad day just like we have good days and bad days. So sometimes it gives you amazing responses and sometimes it doesn't. Sometimes you're using the same prompt and your answers that you get back from it are different and that's OK. That's perfectly OK. All you have to do is reenter it or open a brand-new chat.

Here it came up with five different ideas. Feel free to read them. And again, if you plug in this prompt within ChatGpt right now you might get different answers and that's Ok, but these are the five that I got.

I took these five and then we went in and said, *"Hey now I need a sub headline."* In this case if you look it gives me the headline. It gives me a hook. It gives me two different things and sometimes you might just get a headline. Sometimes you might get one simple response, sometimes it's a very detailed response.

I go into my next thing and say I need sub headlines so I picked one of the headlines from the last response. I liked AI Affiliate Marketing Secrets Unveiled. I said, *"Hey could you please give me a sub headline for this headline."* I copied and pasted the headline: "AI Affiliate Marketing Secrets Unveiled."

If for some reason you don't like any of them, you can hit the regenerate response at the bottom or you can ask it to do it again and ask it to give you 10 different headlines and it'll do that. So, you can pick the one that you like.

I picked one I liked and I asked it to give me a sub headline so it came up with a sub headlines you right here: "Discover the Untapped Potential of AI in Boosting Your Affiliate Marketing Success."

See picture below.

RO   please give me a subheadline for AI Affiliate Marketing Secrets Unveiled

   "Discover the Untapped Potential of AI in Boosting Your Affiliate Marketing Success"

Now you have your headline, and you have a sub headline. You already see all this process could take you 5 minutes.

Now we're going on to the writing the landing page copy. My prompts will be a little bit more detail because now I'm taking the output of the past prompt and making it the input for this prompt. So now I'm saying hey, *"Could you please give me sales copy for my landing page."*

In the past I didn't give it a tone but now that and writing the copy piece; the actual copy for our paragraph for the landing page, I'm going to give it the tone that I wanted. I'd like it to keep the tone fun, informational and exciting. That's just the way I like the talk. Feel free to use it: fun, informational and exciting. You're getting excitement going, it's informational and you get people's attention. Those are the three tones I use all the time for my sales copywriting. It makes it so that the response that you get is not very robotic. Otherwise, when we don't give it a tone sometimes responses come back very robotic and then people just figure that it's not human written content. So, this is your differentiator right here. You give it a tone.

I also gave it the headline and the sub headline that I picked from my last two prompts. So they said my headline is: and I copied and pasted that. So go ahead if you want copy and paste this or plug your headlines, plug in your sub headline that you like into this. And change your tone if you want to change your tone.

Could you please give me a sales copy for my landing page using the headline: AI Affiliate Marketing Secrets Unveiled, the subheadline: Discover the Untapped Potential of AI in Boosting Your Affiliate Marketing Success and keep the tone fun, informational and exciting

This was my prompt for to create the sales page:

If you want it to sound serious or in your talking style, plug this into ChatGpt and then it comes back with this amazing sales page copy. It gives you the headline, the sub headline, the paragraph, and a call to action. Isn't that amazing!

You can now build your landing page based off of this or you can take this and give it to your website person and say if you're hiring somebody to build your website or landing page you can give them this. A lot of times people that make websites are not copywriters. OK so just because they could do the technical website piece doesn't mean that they can do the marketing or copywriting.

Yet here's your copyright. You don't have to hire a copyrighter. Here it is.

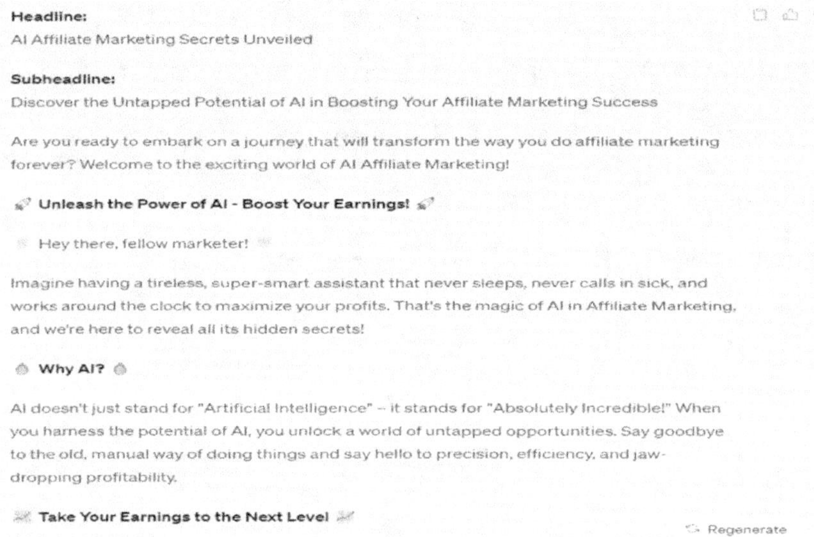

Headline:
AI Affiliate Marketing Secrets Unveiled

Subheadline:
Discover the Untapped Potential of AI in Boosting Your Affiliate Marketing Success

Are you ready to embark on a journey that will transform the way you do affiliate marketing forever? Welcome to the exciting world of AI Affiliate Marketing!

Unleash the Power of AI - Boost Your Earnings!

Hey there, fellow marketer!

Imagine having a tireless, super-smart assistant that never sleeps, never calls in sick, and works around the clock to maximize your profits. That's the magic of AI in Affiliate Marketing, and we're here to reveal all its hidden secrets!

Why AI?

AI doesn't just stand for "Artificial Intelligence" – it stands for "Absolutely Incredible!" When you harness the potential of AI, you unlock a world of untapped opportunities. Say goodbye to the old, manual way of doing things and say hello to precision, efficiency, and jaw-dropping profitability.

Take Your Earnings to the Next Level

Regenerate

However, you got to make sure that it makes sense. It must read well and connect with you. If it connects with you, it's probably going to connect with your audience. Once it does that you can give this to your website person and say make me a landing page with this or you could use this input and build your own landing page using programs like Click Funnels. How easy it is. In less than 10 minutes you can get all of this stuff created and then plug it in to your landing page and boom right you have a landing page like how amazing and cool that is.

I'll give you this bonus trick that sometimes it comes back with a long landing page copy. We've seen the trend that the shorter the copy the shorter the page sometimes it converts better. So, this is the trick, I sometimes go back in ChatGpt and say make it shorter, can you please make it longer, can you elaborate on that or can you explain it a little bit more. That way you can control the length of the output.

What happens next? You have to do a thank you page copy. Copy this prompt on ChatGpt and say *"Hey could you please give me a copy for a thank you page for a product that's called AI Affiliate Marketing [now again you're gonna put in your product] in there that you're promoting."*

Again I'm going to put in the tone because anytime I'm writing paragraphs, I want to give a tone so it doesn't sound so robotic. I add in keep the tone fun, informational and exciting because those are the three that I use most of the time.

Once you put that in it comes back with a thank you page. It puts it in this beautiful format: gives you the headline, the paragraph, sub headline, the thank you for joining; that's very important and even the called to action to register for community.

If any part of this that you don't feel like you really need, don't want the paragraph, not a big fan of the way it read, then you can go in and change that manually. But now you're not staring at a blank piece of paper or a blank screen. This cut down so much time.

Now you can take this copy and put it in your thank you page within your funnels and boom your lead magnet page is completed and your thank you page completed all within 15 minutes.

That's the power of AI and how fast you can go if you use the AI tools properly. This was your landing page creation. The Next secret we're also going to be talking about is designing ads with AI. I'm excited and I'm looking forward to seeing you or your landing pages

Chapter 2 Secret #2 How to Design Ads with AI

In this secret we are going to be covering ad design. What type of tool can you use to create your ad design. Because you're going to have these amazing products which are the foundation of your business.

Let's say create social media ad copy and image ideas using AI. So, think of what type of image should that ad copy come up with. All of this is here the fast track your ad creation process.

OK so what type of prompts do you need? We're gonna start off with ChatGpt again. That's the starting point. We use ChatGpt because it's free. This is the free version that we're using. You could also use tools like Jasper all sorts of things all different types of other tools that are coming out for AI content creation. You can also use the paid version if you want but the prompt that I'm using is the free version of ChatGPT. It works just fine so feel free to use the free version for the ad copy.

For the ad copy, you can ask it something like this: "Please help me write ad copy for Facebook that will capture the attention of customers who are interested in [insert your product] and encourage them to buy my affiliate marketing product." Where it says Facebook you can go in there and change that to IG you could do Google. So that's very interchangeable if it's the same prompt. And once you copy and paste this within ChatGpt, you get this amazing copy. It tells you what the opening should be, what the hook should be, what are the benefits and the call to action.

The majority of the time when people write an ad, they forget about the call to action. They give you a call to action because you're going to ask them to do something; to take some sort of action. It's writing for you; it's telling you what it should be. And if you're not happy with the copy it's OK to hit the regenerator button. Then it comes back with another ad copy.

Then you could say I like that ad copy, but I also need an image idea. I'm using the same chat window because I'm having this conversation with the ChatGpt. It created this ad copy for me. Now I go back in there and ask: please help me create a MidJourney prompt to come up with a graphics for this ad copy.

MidJourney is a tool that does for pictures what ChatGpt does for written content. It creates amazing AI images. You can use a prompt like "Imagine a captivating image that perfectly complement your [insert your affiliate product]. MidJourney or even Canva. Canva not only helps you create social media graphics and other graphics, but it also can generate AI images so you can copy and paste your prompt there.

They're also other free image generating tools that you can copy this prompt there and generate the ideas for your ad. Now you know exactly how you would structure your ads both with their written copy as well as your graphics. All of this takes you about 15 Max 20 minutes. You're so far ahead so fast. I love how fast everything moves if you use the proper tool. These are the tools, the prompts that you use to get ahead and move super fast during your ad creation. Let's keep moving.

Chapter 3 Secret #3 Using AI Email Series

This secret we are going to be covering how to use AI tools to create follow up emails. This is the part that gets missed the majority of the time in affiliate marketing. People often do not follow up with the leads they collect and get overwhelmed by how to write the e-mail. So, I want to show you how to use the AI tools again to get this process going and make it super-fast.

Now what type of e-mail follow up can you write with AI? we're gonna use ChatGPT. Again, as the free version. We're going to be able to write the welcome e-mail series and e-mail broadcast. Once you have an e-mail address then you can write the welcome e-mail that gives them the free thing, the lead magnet that you promised them that you would give them, and you can write broadcast emails. Thus, if you have other affiliate products that match the same e-mail list, you can promote those products through broadcast e-mails.

The process is the same for both the welcome email and broadcast emails. here's the first prompt for the e-mail series. I said, *"Can you please write a welcome e-mail for my product called AI filiated marketing."* This was for the welcome email. The prompt for the broadcast email is very similar. When you're writing the broadcast e-mail, just tweak it. Instead of saying welcome e-mail you're just going to say, *"Could you please help me write an e-mail promoting this product [and then write the product name and describe what the product is what does]."* That's all the difference between the two prompts. One is the welcome e-mail and the product name, the other is the promotion e-mail for the product with a little description of what it does.

You can get that description from the landing page. Once you've entered this prompt into ChatGpt it will come back with a response. It's going to give you the subject line and the copy for what the e-mail should be. It welcomes you, it gives what's in store for you, what we have plan; a lot of detail.

However, the welcome e-mail, I like to keep it concise; to fit in this one screen shot. Sometimes like I said, AI has good days and bad days just like we do. So if it's a really long, in the same chat window, I'll prompt it and say, "hey this is great but could you make it shorter." I want it to give me a much shorter version of that same welcome e-mail.

Perhaps you don't like the subject line, you can go back in there just like having a chat with ChatGPT and say make it shorter or could you give me 10 more recommendations for the subject line. It's going to give you 10 more options.

Remember this is a chat tool you're having a conversation with AI. So, your prompts don't have to be complicated. Don't make it so overwhelming that you don't know where to start. Do you see the results from these easy, clean prompts?

Another tip, what I normally do is give it a tone. I say make the tone fun, informational, and educational. You could put that in. Let's say you forgot tone and really don't like the way the e-mail looks. In the same chat series, you can still go back and say could you please make the tone of this e-mail fun and exciting. You can put the tone even after it gives you a response. You don't have to rewrite the prompt again. It will rewrite the same e-mail with that new tone. Then you'll see that it starts flowing much better.

For the broadcast series, it's the same concept.

The same prompt applies. You just tell it what you're promoting you have to give that information where you just tell it what you're promoting and a little bit more detail about it. That's it. Prompt ChatGpt, *"Give me a promotional e-mail for: [this product and give it a little bit more detail about what the product is.]"* It's going to spit that out. If you don't like the way it looks, you can add a little bit more detail. Say, "Hey can you please include you know that this product has [these features or this benefit.]" Then it'll incorporate that within the e-mail.

You have to remember this is a chat, a back-and-forth conversation. So, if you don't like the initial output that you get, you can always go back and  change it. Happy e-mail writing and we'll continue with the next secret.

Chapter 4 Secret #4 AI for SOCIAL MEDIA CONTENT

In this secret we are going to be covering how you're going to create social media content using AItools. Remember

you're going to be driving organic social media traffic to your landing page, to your offers that you're promoting.

You could spend hours and hours trying to create social media content, but we're going to be using AI.

So, what type of social media content can you create with AI?

You can create the content itself so you can come up with ideas of what you should be posting.

You can come up with the actual captions of what the post is about.

And you could also come up with graphic prompts and or ideas even if you're not putting them into a program like MidJourney, Canva or some other program that creates AI graphics.

You could still get ideas of what the graphics should look like and create it yourself.

Let's dive in. I'm excited.

For the social media content, the first prompt I am going to put in to ChatGPT is *"Can you please help me come up with 10 IG post ideas about how to use AI tools for [insert your affiliate marketing product]."*

If you're promoting an offer on weight loss it should say give me 10 ideas about tips on how to lose weight in a healthy way or exercise tips or whatever your industry or niche. I said IG post ideas, you can say Facebook post ideas, LinkedIn post ideas whatever platform. Also, I said 10 ideas and it doesn't have to be 10 it could be 5, 15 or 20. I stick with 10 it gives me enough ideas and just because it gives me this it does not mean I have to use all ten. I pick and choose.

AI has good and it has bad days just like we have good days. Sometimes it gives me the post idea and it breaks down the post for me. It may give me relevant hashtags and emojis. It doesn't do that all the time. If it does it for you amazing. If it doesn't, it still gives ideas so that's ok.

Let's say they only gives you 10 different ideas; just like one liners. How are you going to create the post? How are you going to write the caption for it? This is the possible prompt to use to write captions. We can say *"Can you please write an IG caption for me an IG, Facebook or LinkedIn caption for unleash the power of AI and then discover how AI tool can supercharge [insert your affiliate marketing product.]"*

I put in the tone now because it's a social media posts, I want it to be a little witty. I add make a tone fun witty and informational because I always like to put information out there.

I put that into ChatGPT and it gave me a beautiful post with lots of emojis and hashtags. I'm like this is great! How fast was that. How much time it saved. How much longer would it take if you had to come up with this on your own. You don't have to worry about any of that. Here you go. It's done for you within like 5 minutes. So now you got ideas for days, right?

Next, we're going to go in and come up with a graphic idea. I have a post, I'm gonna need a graphic. You can even make it into a video too. If you don't want to put a graphic, you can actually read this; talk it in your own voice if you wanted to and create a video or make a reel. Then you don't have to worry about graphics.

But I'm gonna come up with graphic ideas. I wrote the caption for it now let's come up with ideas for graphics. I said *"Can you please write an IG caption for me on IG, Facebook or LinkedIn graphic ideas for unleash the power of AI and then discover how AI tool can supercharge [insert your affiliate marketing product.]"*

It came up with these five amazing ideas. And I said maybe do a lightning bolt or supercharged lightning bolts or rocket launch. Kind of describe what those were. If you have a graphics person pick the one that you like and say hey, make me graphic that looks like this. If you don't have a graphic person, you at least have an idea of what put into your free version of Canva and make something similar.

Remember, you can interchange prompts. Just because I showed you this process doesn't mean you have to follow it exactly. You could say I don't even want to create this myself. I just want AI to create the graphics so you could use that in MidJourney or Canva. And again, there's so many other tools that do graphic generation using AI. You could post that prompt in their program and let AI create it for you.

Now you have at least two different options both for ad and graphics using AI. This cuts down your time so much of this can be done within a day. You can have your business pretty much up and running in one day. You're affiliate marketing business and new product and go through this process within one day. You can have your page running, your landing page, your emails completed, social media posts, ad design and graphics created. That was unheard of in the past, but now you have all these amazing tools that can help you do just that.

Chapter 5 Next Steps

I'm so excited to see all the amazing content that you're going to be creating for your affiliate marketing promotions using AI.

Also, how fast you can turn these things out. If something doesn't work, then you know you could create something different.

I have a few forwarding thoughts that are going to help you in your journey.

The first thing is to make your voice your own voice. I realize that we just studied the use of AI. I know a lot of people say that it sounds robotic. And you're saying well how is this my voice if I'm using AI. You can train AI. Remember how we put in the tones that we wanted it the sound like. So, you can tell AI to sound like you. To do that you're going to have to figure out how you sound. You can record yourself or write a couple of paragraphs and you can send that in to ChatGpt and say I write like this. Can you please analyze the tone that i use or write like my writing style. You can tell it to do that and then it gets trained on your writing style on your voice. Now suddenly it doesn't sound like a robot it sounds like you.

It's scary. I know it's creepy and scary. I get it, but you're using it to your advantage. If you don't do that you are going to be left behind because everything is getting created so fast these days.

If you want to do it your traditional way, then that's Ok. You can. I mean do you have to use AI? Absolutely not. You can do it your own way but everything else is gonna move so fast that you must work extra hard trying to keep up with all those things.

Train it to your way. It's not going to be you. You know it's not you. Make sure you check it don't just copy and paste blindly. Check it. Always read what it writes back make sure you proofread. Even if you had a ghost writer write for you, you're still going to read it to make sure that it sounds like you; your story; your voice. The same logic applies. Use it as a ghost writer. Use it like a tool, but you still are the main person that everything filters through.

Train it in your own voice or if it comes back with something different, use it inspiration, and convert it to your own ways. That's going to be your difference maker and that's how you're going to succeed.

The next thing: you created one piece of content and you're gonna say why am I not making sales. You must be consistent. You can't just do a thing, one time and expect to see results. These things take time. You're gonna have to do it week after week, month after month and sometimes it's gonna take multiple months.

There are people, I'm gonna tell you there are people that first time to try it they had huge success. But they're also people that have been trying for years and have not seen success. Both things happen. However, now with AI tool that years that people have been trying and not making it can be cut down. 2-3 years can now be cut to 2-3 months because of how fast you can move and try different things. If this didn't work, ok let's tweak it. Ok this didn't work this didn't resonate with my audience, let's change the tone, talk to them differently, think of a different angle on how to promote this product. Those are the things that would have taken you years to figure out, but now you can cut that down to weeks or months because you're using AI.

You still must be consistent. Put yourself out there, put content out there, build your e-mail list, get your offers out there, and see the benefits of affiliate marketing.

Make your own voice and start thinking outside the box. Just because somebody does it this way doesn't mean you have to do it the same way. You could do it other ways. I gave you a bunch of ideas, different prompts. Mix and match, think outside the box.

Think of your own prompts. If you were looking for some sort of content, how would you ask it. I gave you a couple of ways how I ask and that's the response I get. I like them. You might not like the response I get because you're not me. You're your own voice.

So, ask it in your way and the AI is going to react to you the way you ask it. Use the ideas that we went through in this course. Use the prompts and see how they were structured.

No need to overcomplicate it or keep telling it to think like this and pretend to be that. If you want to, if that's what makes sense to you then yes by all means do it. if it doesn't make sense to you, do it this way.

Connect the dots. If something's working in another industry, like if you like the headline of from a billboard ad that you saw or headline on some TikTok videos, you want to combine with yours.

It can be a completely different industry and you could use that. You can use inspiration not copying. Use it as inspiration for a different industry in a different way to boost your prompts. Say, *"Hey I like this copy could you write something similar for this product, for this industry."*

These are the things that's gonna make you successful. You must make your own voice, you have to be consistent, and you have to start thinking outside the box. Because if you just follow your not gonna make your own way.

I hope this book really helped you. I am expecting that it accelerates and cut your journey down from years to weeks. Now you can put your content out so much faster. I'm looking forward to seeing all the different things that you come up with.

I'm so excited I wish you the best and happy affiliate marketing using this wonderful AI tool.